LOS ANGELES

Designed and Produced by

Ted Smart & David Gibbon

MAYFLOWER BOOKS · NEW YORK CITY

Introduction ~ The Many-hearted City

IT is often said that Los Angeles is a city without a real heart, that central area in every large city in which its government, entertainment quarter, shopping areas and so on are contained: the hub which is the focus point of the city's life. There is some truth to this view, for Los Angeles has grown so rapidly in the decades since World War II that it cannot compare with world cities of comparable size that have had centuries in which to develop.

Another view is that Los Angeles is a city with several hearts, all beating powerfully in their respective locations and sending the lifeblood of the city coursing along the circulatory system of the freeways in a helter-skelter of vehicles with people who scurry about the city on business or pleasure.

This, too, is true and one glance at a map of the city, which stretches like a gargantuan tadpole – its head reaching over the Santa Monica Mountains into the San Fernando Valley to the north and its tail wiggling its way south to the port of Los Angeles and Long Beach – will instantly reveal the diffuse nature of the community.

The historical eye of this monster's head is a small plaza with the unexpected atmosphere of an old Spanish village. This is where the Pueblo de Nuestra Senora la Reina de Los Angeles (the town of Our Lady, the Queen of the Angels) was founded by the Spaniards. Neglected for many years, the Pueblo has now become part of an area of 42 acres preserved as a State Historical landmark.

In the center of the square rises an old bandstand of the kind found in Latin American villages, around which the inhabitants usually promenade during summer evenings. The same traditions are maintained in this quiet area of Los Angeles, almost the only place free of traffic. Bands play during the summer evenings and colorful Mexican fiestas are celebrated with mariachi groups filling the air with the sounds of guitars and providing a feast for the eye with their romantic Mexican sombreros and embroidered ponchos.

One of the oldest buildings in the Plaza is the old Mission Church, now known as the Plaza Church. This is one of a string of churches and missions built along the coast by the Spaniards in an attempt to colonize California. The Plaza Church began as a chapel for the settlers in 1784 and was rebuilt in 1822 on the proceeds of the sale of several barrels of wine donated by the San Gabriel mission. Even that money was not enough to erect more than a very simple structure and over the years the weather has taken its toll on the adobe walls. There has been some restoration however, and in the interior much of the spirit which comforted and inspired the early settlers remains. The altar is of carved wood inset with paintings, and the painted ceiling and wooden pews are reminders of churches in old Spain. With the tall palms growing in its courtyard and its rebuilt belltower with three bells set in arches, the Church has retained for Los Angeles the character of its early days.

The lonely splendor of the coastline at sunset previous page *is sharply contrasted with the busy Harbor Freeway* left *as it by-passes the City Center.*

Another attractive reminder of the city's Spanish origins is found at Olvera Street. Here is the oldest house in Los Angeles, the Avila Adobe, built in the original village in 1818, and the feeling of the street market that ran along the old main street is still to be found here today. Olvera Street is for pedestrians only; small shops with craftsmen at work line the street and musicians stroll amid the stalls on which hang embroidered shirts, scarves and leather belts, or step carefully around the piles of pottery displayed on the sidewalk. In the evenings, the lanterns glow and music fills the air, as do the odors of tacos and enchiladas which visitors order at take-out stalls or enjoy at the Mexican restaurants.

In the Pueblo there are also buildings from the city's early American period when rich ranchers put up at the Pico House, the grandest hotel of its day boasting three stories and eight rooms, some with an article of bathroom furniture which was a novelty in the West in 1869 – a bathtub with hot water. There is also the Merced Theater where gala nights were packed with everyone of note in old Los Angeles.

In complete contrast to the Pueblo but close by it across the Hollywood Freeway, is the modern Civic Center. This complex of buildings is in a spacious area with parks and malls green with palms and evergreens. In it, the city authorities have tried to create that focal point which the city lacks. The buildings are conventionally designed, according to the pattern of other civic centers in the U.S., and a good deal of the city's cultural life revolves about them.

One end is dominated by the City Hall which, until 1957, was the tallest building in the city, rising 32 stories and providing magnificent views on those rare smogless days.

On the western end of the complex is another striking building, the Water and Power Building. This block by Albert C. Martin was built in 1964 and is particularly striking at night when the interior lighting shining through its abundant glass converts it into a huge sparkling cube that dominates the city.

Alongside the Water and Power Building is a black glass and marble building which is at the heart of the musical life of Los Angeles. This is the Dorothy Chandler Pavilion which was built in 1964 and houses the Los Angeles Philharmonic Orchestra. Its auditorium seats 3250 people who attend performances of opera, ballet and music in its modern setting. The Pavilion is one of a trio of buildings for theatrical entertainments. The other two are the Mark Taper Forum, a smaller theater where much experimental drama is performed, and the Ahmanson Theater which can accommodate 2000 people for plays and musical shows.

In the West Coast cities of America the Orient has always had a foothold which was established first when the Chinese arrived to work on the railway which was to link the two oceans that virtually surround the United States. Later, Japanese fruit farmers, attracted by stories of the fruitful valleys of the interior, came over to contribute their expertise in fruit cultivation.

Los Angeles' Chinatown lies to the north of the Pueblo and consists of a two-block area of Chinese buildings with large sloping roofs, covered in bright glazed tiles, pagoda-like towers and colorful signs in Chinese characters advertising the presence of shops, restaurants and food markets. Like Little Tokyo, Los Angeles' second Oriental community which lies to the southeast of the City Hall, Chinatown is popular with the tourists who visit the city. Both areas also have their own commercial life which is part of the city's larger business life.

It is in downtown Los Angeles that major business development has taken place in recent years and here, to the southwest of the Civic Center, the high-rise buildings are beginning to take on the appearance of Italian cities of the Renaissance with their towers trying to outdo each other in height and magnificence. Formerly, this area, known as Bunker Hill, was the place where Los Angeles society resided but as they moved out the neighborhood became run down and is now going through a rebirth as a center of business and shopping.

Its center lies around Pershing Square, named after the World War I General but, surprisingly, possessing a statue of Beethoven, a relic of the days when this was the cultural center of the city and the Philharmonic Auditorium was situated here. Other reminders of the grand old days of this part of the city are the Biltmore Hotel, with its vast and imposing lobby and the murals of Giovanni Smeralda who also decorated Grand Central Station in New York in the nineteen twenties, and the Alexandria Hotel with its Tiffany ceilings which once looked down on everyone of note who visited Los Angeles. Today, both hotels are experiencing the same renaissance as the rest of this section of the city and the old glory has returned, enhanced by the nostalgia for the past felt by many present-day visitors.

Nearby, a startling contrast is provided by the modern Bonaventure Hotel, a vast complex of circular towers looking like the silos of some space station awaiting the arrival of visitors from another planet. Near it are other new giants like the 52-story Arco Plaza building and among them, looking like some Arabian nights castle, the Central Library.

This great storehouse of books, and there are more than four million of them, is the most important in the Western U.S.A. The building in which they are housed is very original, not to say extraordinary, in design. Bernard Goodhue, the architect who built it in 1925, was evidently a man of eclectic taste, for in its design one can identify Byzantine, Egyptian and Aztec influences. The exterior form of the building appears as a castle at street level and ends up as a mosaic-covered tent at the top.

Though purists may regard this type of architecture without much enthusiasm, it nevertheless reflects the spirit of the new society of America where the old cultural values of Europe, imported by a basically untutored population of immigrants, is fused with the energy and dynamism of a people establishing a new world with the roots of the old.

This is the basis of much of the fanciful architecture of that home of fantasy, Hollywood, which in its film sets, its restaurants, burger palaces and even in the homes of the stars themselves, presents a rich mixture of contrasting styles.

The tradition was established early on by film-maker D.W. Griffiths who, in his epic *Intolerance,* mixed Babylonian, Egyptian, Indian and other styles in an epic set which has never been equaled. Today, the architecture of the fantastic is everywhere: in Mann's (formerly Grauman's) Theater where the stars left their hand and footprints in the concrete in front of the strange South Sea Island/Chinese/Mexican-style movie house; in the Brown Derby's hemispherical architecture; or in the innumerable eating houses decked out as Hawaiian huts, Chinese temples or Aztec palaces.

Hollywood, as it deserves, has a chapter to itself in this book, so we therefore turn elsewhere in our search for the fantastic. The neighborhood of Watts, in which resides the majority of L.A.'s black population, was the scene of violent rioting one hot summer not long ago, and also contains one of the most remarkable examples of monumental folk art in the world. This consists of three conical towers built of wire rods and concrete and decorated with ceramics, shells and pieces of glass. It was built singlehandedly by Simon Rodia who dedicated himself to this labor of love for thirty-three years and, having finished it, left Los Angeles and his life's work behind without fuss. At first, the city authorities intended to demolish this folly, but its artistic merit was recognized by the public, who opposed its destruction and saved it for posterity as a truly remarkable city monument.

Just as amazing, though because of its familiarity no one would term it so, is Dodgers Stadium in Elysian Park to the north of the city center. This is the home of the Dodgers baseball team, formerly of Brooklyn. It is a vast diamond whose terraces hold 56,000 seats with unobstructed views of the game. Around the stadium are giant parking lots which can accommodate the cars of the spectators who number more than two and a half million each season.

Sport is an important aspect of Los Angeles life, and one of the places where Los Angelenos exercise is 4064-acre Griffith Park. This is one of the largest city parks in the United States and on a fine weekend is used by over 50,000 people who can ride, hike, listen to music, study the bird life in the Sanctuary or the plants in Fern Dell. All the flora and fauna of the park are on show at the Fern Dell Nature Museum, a favorite starting place for walkers in the vast park and one which vies in popularity with the Los Angeles Zoo, another of the park's attractions.

At the Zoo, the animals are in the open, their freedom limited only by moats and natural obstructions and their habitats are made to resemble those of their native terrains. There is also a children's Zoo, with such attractions as the Prairie Dog Colony, Mouse House and Baby Elephant compound.

Southwest of the hub of the city is another sports center at Exposition Park. Here is the Memorial Coliseum built for the 1932 Olympics, which seats over 100,000 people. The Universities of Los Angeles and California play their football games at the Coliseum and there are track meets and other shows such as rodeos and parades. Nearby is an indoor Sports Arena where boxing matches, tennis championships, basketball games, and other events take place.

Leisure pursuits of Los Angelenos are not solely devoted to sporting activity, however, and on any weekend the museums are full of people. The Museum of Art, built in 1965, is one of the largest in the U.S.A. and is built over the tar pits in Hancock Park, an area where the bones of prehistoric creatures who died in the pits have been found and recreated in lifelike models. Although a newcomer to the world of art collections, the Museum has some fine paintings and sculptures, including the dramatic Rodin statue of Balzac. Other collections are the result of private patronage. For example, the Huntington Library, which has one of the largest collections of rare books and manuscripts in the world, was bequeathed to the public by H.E. Huntington, a tycoon and collector of both art and books. One of the few copies of the famous Gutenberg Bible is here and so is a first folio of Shakespeare. There are also some fine examples of British eighteenth-century painters, such as Lawrence and Gainsborough.

Another extraordinary private collection is the one left by J. Paul Getty, popularly thought of as the richest man in the world. The Getty Collection at Santa Monica specializes in Greek and Roman sculpture and Dutch and Italian painters. There are also tapestries and furniture in this million-dollar museum and a fullsize model of the Villa dei Papyri which was unearthed from the ashes in which it was buried at Herculaneum following the eruption of Vesuvius in AD 79.

Whether by chance or because of its association with the motion picture industry, Los Angeles and its surrounding country are abundantly supplied with unusual or off-beat entertainments and attractions. Many of these are scattered about the rambling city; most are easily accessible if not centrally situated. Among them are farms and animal breeding establishments, mock villages of the Old West, botanical gardens and one of the world's most famous observatories.

To the northwest, on the outer edges of the city and on the San Diego Freeway, are the Busch Gardens, a beautiful park with lakes on which one can take boat trips and view waterfalls and exotic aquatic birds. There are endless sideshows besides and one of the unusual excursions is a monorail tour of the Anheuser Busch brewery which owns the park.

Farther east lie the San Gabriel mountains. Atop Mount Wilson is the famous Observatory, with its powerful 100-inch Hooker telescope camera which has probed into millions of light years of space in an effort to unravel the mystery of the universe.

Directly below the mountain lie the Arboretum Botanical Gardens, created on an old ranch and now a horticultural center, and the California Institute of Technology, which is one of the world's leading educational establishments for science and engineering.

To get to these places of leisure or, indeed, to their work Los Angelenos must commute.

The scattered nature of the city of Los Angeles, which overlaps into the county of Los Angeles and surrounding counties, has led to the development of a sophisticated freeway system providing rapid travel from one area of Los Angeles to another. This has encouraged 90% of Los Angelenos to use their own vehicles instead of public transport, and has created traffic problems of considerable proportions which the administration has had to deal with by providing still more freeways and parking facilities.

Few homes in Los Angeles city are farther than four miles from a freeway and the traffic is intense. Moreover, Los Angeles receives over 20 million people a year through its international airport, who add to the already high number of urban travelers.

Traffic is just one problem which has grown out of the successful industrial and business development of the city. Others are sewage and waste disposal, but worse than either of these is smog.

It is ironic that one of the reasons why two of Los Angeles' major industries moved to the county was because it had clear air and sunshine. For the film industry, this meant the economy of location shooting instead of having to make expensive indoor sets; for the aircraft industry it provided ideal conditions for flying and testing aircraft. Today, they would both choose somewhere else to go, for the combination of fumes from factory chimneys and the hot sun produces a smog for which Los Angeles is notorious.

The effect of the smog on the health of the population has been severe, causing an increase in cardiac deaths and in lung diseases, while agriculture, already reduced by the take-over of farming land by urban development, has decreased.

With the prospect of the population continuing to increase into the 1980s the administration is concerned that the city should not suffer irreparable damage from the circumstances in which it finds itself. But the administration has problems of its own.

The administrative structure of the city and county is a tangled web of overlapping agencies which confuse the lines of authority and, therefore, action. In many cases the city has duplicated services, while in other cases departments are almost autonomous. In these circumstances, the city's development is too much the result of the enterprise of individuals who put profit before the interests of the community as a whole. Too often this has led to the despoiling of the countryside in such formerly beautiful areas as the Santa Monica Mountains and the San Fernando Valley.

In time, if Los Angeles continues to exist, it may become a city in the traditional European sense, but even the great cities have been subjected to extensive destruction and rebuilding to give them the form in which we see them today. Paris, for example, was rebuilt by Henry IV as well as by Napoleon and Baron Haussman. In Los Angeles, the threat of destruction is ever-present with the San Andreas fault, a major cause of earthquakes, a mere 30 miles away from the city center. Perhaps it is this as much as anything else that gives Los Angeles a slightly transient character, as if the population might at any moment move away as quickly as it arrived, and endows it with a talent for living in the present with an intensity that is wholly its own.

Traffic makes its way along Western Avenue overleaf between the timeless palm-trees and the modern buildings of Los Angeles.

Flanking a beautiful fountain lagoon, the magnificent Dorothy Chandler Pavilion right, the Ahmanson Theater above and the Mark Taper Forum bottom right overleaf comprise the Los Angeles Music Center for the Performing Arts which is considered to be one of the world's finest cultural centers.

The City Hall, once the tallest building in Southern California, can be seen left behind the pretty peacock fountain and below in the background of the Civic Center Mall.

Situated in the heart of movietown, on the famous Hollywood and Vine above, is the circular Capitol Records building below, its famous 92-foot phonograph needle soaring high into the sky.

The vital city skyline excites the imagination by night above left and overleaf, while left is shown the daytime bustle on busy Alvarado Street.

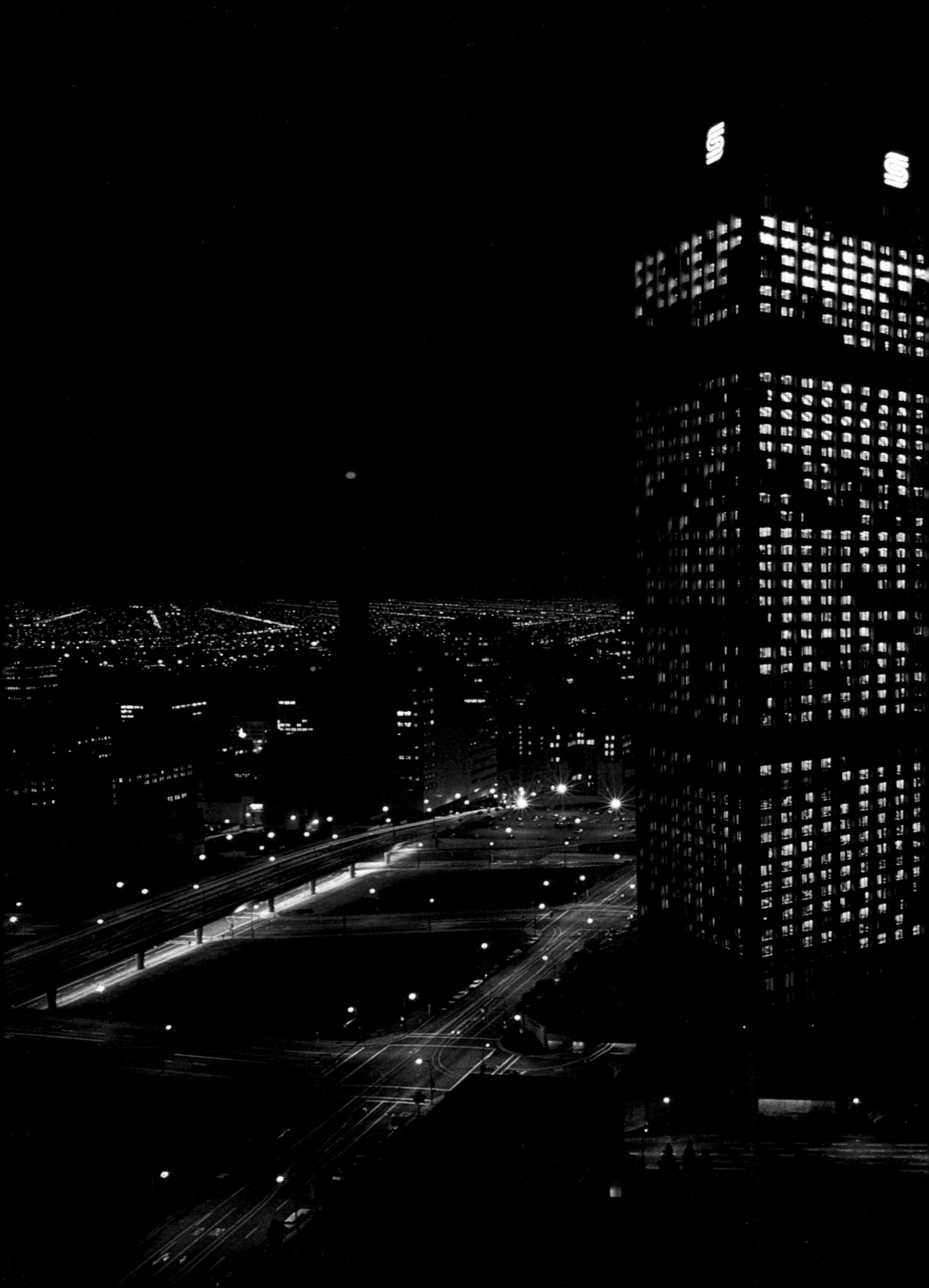

Fascinating Chinatown, created in the Eastern image above, below and center left, *features picturesque pagodas* above and far right ornamented with balconies and gold trim.

Sited on Hollywood Boulevard below is Mann Chinese Theater right *where the footprints and autographs of Hollywood's 'greats' are immortalized in concrete.*

Traffic pulses along the Harbor Freeway in Downtown L.A. overleaf.

From Colony to Cowtown and Metropolis

THE story of Los Angeles begins in 1769 when Gaspar de Portola, during his journey of exploration along the west coast of America, camped at a small river which he named El Rio de Nuestra Senora La Reina de Los Angeles de Porciuncula. Portola moved on and left the job of colonization to Felipe de Neve, the Governor of the Spanish Province, who created a small settlement by introducing 22 adults and 22 children into the region whose only other outpost of civilization was the mission built by Franciscan fathers at San Gabriel.

Despite the epic stories of the opening of the West, it appears that the colonizing of uninhabited territory did not stir many adventurous spirits, for the first inhabitants of Los Angeles were mostly Indians and blacks, persuaded or perhaps even obliged by the priests and the authorities to found the settlement. This small community soon discovered that the climate and soil of their new land was remarkably productive of grain, and that the vast empty acres were suitable for cattle and horse breeding as well.

Stories of the richness of the soil began to percolate over the mountains and were spread by the sailors who frequented the West Coast, despite the Spanish laws prohibiting trade with foreigners. The Spaniards had other problems to cope with anyway, as their American Empire began to crumble under the pressure of movements for independence among the colonists. In Mexico, this came in 1821 and for a few years Los Angeles became part of Mexico.

The influx of Americans had already begun, led by men like Joseph Chapman, a piratical character from the East Coast. Chapman was also a master carpenter and among his contributions to the community was his work in the church that now stands in the Plaza of the Pueblo. Jedediah Smith, who arrived overland from Missouri, was another pioneer. He was a hunter and trapper and was followed by others like him who came to explore the golden land of which they had heard.

Meanwhile, the new Mexican Government and the people who were settling in the West had found that their interests conflicted, and war broke out in 1846. Los Angeles was quickly occupied by Commodore Stockton and surrendered without resistance. Shortly thereafter, the townspeople rallied, driving out the American troops who headed north for Monterey where they were later joined by General Kearney's force which had also suffered a reverse at San Pasqual. Together, Stockton and Kearney decided to attack Los Angeles again and they took it in January, 1847.

Two years later, gold was discovered in the Sierra Nevada to the north and life in Los Angeles took a new course. The sudden increase in the population of San Francisco, the gateway to the gold fields, created a demand for food which the Los Angelenos ranchers were able to supply and which turned the rural community into a busy and rowdy cattle town.

Bathed in sunshine the City Hall left is seen from L.A.'s famous flag plaza, where all the flags that have ever been flown over the city are proudly displayed.

The overflow of people from the north attracted by prospects of easy money caused overcrowding and Los Angeles became a lawless city where crime and vice were rampant. As in San Francisco, murder became an everyday event and prostitution a thriving industry. The feverish life of the town erupted finally in a massacre of Chinese for the accidental killing of a white man, but this also marked the beginning of the end of the era of unbridled violence.

By the time the transcontinental railway arrived from Chicago via Santa Fe, life had become more stable and, according to the advertisements of the railway companies eager to find passengers, full of promise for new arrivals. 'Go West, young man' became the admonition of Easterners to their youth, and West they came, taking advantage of the cheap fares offered by the railway companies that in their rivalry had reduced the cost of the journey from one hundred dollars to ten and, on occasions, less.

The new arrivals, who included farmers from the Midwest, turned to exploiting the rich land, developing the orchards started by the Spanish fathers. Soon there was a steady flow of fruit from west to east on the railroads that had brought the new settlers. The wild old days of ranchers who rode the ranges and raised hell in the city on Saturday nights were fading rapidly. Instead there was a new generation of sober, hardworking citizens who expanded the city.

Two new developments now changed the destiny of Los Angeles once more; one was the discovery of oil and the other the acquisition of the coastal town of San Pedro which was developed as an artificial harbor. The oil wells proliferated where now there are buildings, particularly round the La Brea Pits, and the oil paid for the work of developing the port area which now made Los Angeles an important seaport as well as an industrial city.

The most important development of all, however, and the one that put Los Angeles firmly on the world map, was the arrival of the film industry just before World War I. It was hardly an industry to start with, merely a handful of enthusiasts cranking cameras in the clear Californian sunshine, but after World War I the expansion of film-making, aided by improved techniques and equipment, was explosive.

The city of angels certainly seems to have been blessed with an extraordinary series of means for survival, for no sooner has one phase of commercial life begun to fade than another has taken its place. When World War II broke out, only a very far-sighted seer would have prophesied the shrinkage of the film industry which television has caused. But while Hollywood slowly became part of a legendary past other important industries of the future were evolving. One of the most important of these is the manufacture of the famous Douglas aircraft that are found in the fleets of many of the world's great airlines; another is the development of electronic equipment.

With its new industries as well as those which have already taken root, Los Angeles looks set for still more growth and prosperity.

...lecting the spirit of Old Mexico, Olvera Street ...se pages was the birthplace of the Los Angeles ...blo and is now maintained as a traffic-free ...xican market with colorful shops, stalls and ...s. Craftsmen such as glass-blowers, ...ersmiths, leather artisans, potters and ...dlemakers display their merchandise in an ...osphere heavy with perfume and spices.

...the tiny open-fronted cafés visitors can enjoy ...hentic Mexican food — tacos and frijoles among ...most popular — quickly prepared and at a low ...

Wilshire Boulevard shown above, left and
above left is one of the world's most exciting
thoroughfares. From a nest of high rise buildings in
Downtown Los Angeles the roadway twists and
curves through the splendors of MacArthur Park and
continues its way past a variety of unusual architect[...]
until it reaches the ocean front at Santa Monica's
Palisades Park.

Situated on Wilshire Boulevard is the original Brow[...]
Derby Restaurant below which traces its origins ba[...]
to 1926, to a hot-dog stand owned by Larry Anders[...]
the second husband of Gloria Swanson. Intimate
dining-rooms, built hacienda-style, lead off the main
dining-room which is shaped like the interior of a la[...]
derby. Guests can choose from a varied menu, includ[...]
a gourmet sea-food salad, dining by the soft glow of
candlelight.

In Pershing Square right the careful landscape
planning provides some of the loveliest blossom displ[...]
during most of the year. Poinsettias bloom during the
holiday period and in the winter months pansies, an[...]
the spectacular birds of paradise, which are the offici[...]
flower of the city, can be seen in profusion.

In a blaze of lights the Harbor Freeway overleaf sk[...]
the spangled skyscrapers of Downtown L.A.

*...mortalized in song, beautiful MacArthur Park,
...atured* on these pages, *was named after the
...mous Second World War General and is
...agnificently landscaped with subtropical
...antings and palms. Dividing the park's superb
...ke is the twenty-mile long Wilshire Boulevard
...hich gracefully curves through the palms and
...liage on its way to the coast.*

*...un-dappled and tranquil, away from the roar of
...e traffic, the park provides a quiet oasis and a
...elcome respite from the day's busy activity.*

*...or children, however, the adventure play area
...bove and left provides fun and excitement as
...ey clamber eagerly to sail — just one more time —
...own the slide, scale the top of the climbing frame
...soar high on the swings.*

The Land of Oz

IN Los Angeles county the land of amazing happenings is not a fiction but a reality invented by many ingenious minds. You need no yellow brick road to discover the bizarre and fantastic, for most freeways and State highways will take you easily to places that cause most of their visitors to gasp with amazement and excitement.

Most of the show-places have plenty of visitors, for more than nine million people come to L.A. every year to enjoy the sunshine and the entertainment, and the money they spend helps provide the capital to create more and more wonders for the world's most ambitious amusement parks.

One of the most breathtaking amusements is provided by a roller coaster aptly called the Great American Revolution. This three-quarters-of-a-mile ride takes its screaming, or tongue-tied passengers on an astonishing high speed journey which includes a 90-feet-high vertical loop. The Revolution is just one of the attractions at Magic Mountain Pleasure Park near Valencia on the Golden State Freeway to the northwest of Los Angeles. Other dizzy entertainments here include such 'pleasures' as a ride down a log flume with a plunge into a lake, and a journey on a runaway train. Quieter activities include an aerial gondola ride through the park.

The Old West with all its aura of adventure and romance is a natural theme for L.A. entertainment parks. With memories of the John Ford and Henry Hathaway action movies still in people's minds, if not on their TV screens, places like Knotts Berry Farm at Buena Park to the east of Los Angeles are highly successful at involving their visitors in 'real life' movie action.

In Knotts Berry Farm's Old West Ghost Town visitors can stroll down the main street in High Noon style, board a stagecoach, pan for gold, and even get involved in a real Jesse James-style hold-up on the Rio Grand Calico Railway.

Indians and Mexicans, indispensable to any scenario of the Old West, can be found at Buena Park, where most summer evenings end with a Mexican firework display which has all the verve of old-time bandits' raids on a frontier town. By way of contrast, Buena Park also has other, more modern amusements. There is an amusement park in which parachute jumps and a Corkscrew roller coaster with two huge loops give visitors a more unusual view of the earth than the one to which they are accustomed. And in the Enchanted Village animals are 'trained by kindness'. Visitors may be startled by the sight of a real live tarantula alighting on someone, or a python wrapping its coils around another 'victim'. The people being so 'attacked' are, of course, attendants and one assumes that the creatures have been trained by them not to bite or squeeze too hard – or at all!

The Hollywood Wax Museum and Movieworld are movie-linked showplaces, the former providing visitors with an opportunity to examine, at their leisure, the stars they hope to, but almost certainly will not, see in real life in Hollywood. At the Wax Museum they can compensate a little for their disappointment and gaze, if not at the real Butch Cassidy and the Sundance Kid, at least at a three-dimensional representation. At Movieworld there are the movie stars' cars; the Mercedes Benz that belonged to Al Jolson, the coach from *Gone with the Wind,* as well as other memorabilia from famous movies.

If the main characteristic of most of these shows around Los Angeles is, like the movies themselves, their ability to persuade the spectator that the fantasies are almost true to life, then surely the most 'characteristic' of all Los Angeles' fun parks, and rivaled only by its counterpart in Florida, must be Disneyland. Here is a world where extraordinarily vivid projections of the imagination made possible by modern technology overlap with the experiences of everyday reality, and it sometimes becomes difficult to distinguish one from the other.

Of all the show-places none is so famous or so totally persuasive as Disneyland, which is 27 miles south of Los Angeles at Anaheim. This superb kingdom of fantasy linked to technology was created twenty years ago by Walt Disney, whose ambition was to make a world where the characters of his brilliant cartoons would have a three-dimensional reality.

The park is divided into six themes and there is so much to see and do in each that no-one would attempt to see all of them in one visit, unless on the guided tour which takes visitors on a sampling trip around them all. For extended visits, there are hotels nearby and it is easy to imagine addicts spending their entire L.A. vacation at the park.

Turning back the time machine, Disneyland offers a trip to old Louisiana where the glamor and mystery of the old French city is evoked, and there is a haunted house full of ghosts, disembodied heads and other phantasmagoria ending with the gathering of the ghosts at a haunted ballroom where they eerily dance the night away.

Still in the past but more robust is the Frontier Days Kingdom with Davy Crockett and other kings of the wild frontier, and the youthful adventures of Mark Twain's famous character Tom Sawyer, which bring to life great days on the Mississippi.

Naturally the future features in the Disney Kingdom, with rides through space, Moon visits and submarine voyages. More earthly adventures are lived out in the jungle boat ride through swamps full of alligators, hippos and other denizens of the waterways, and on a safari with lions and elephants to confront.

For some people, particularly for the young in heart, the most joyous section of Disneyland is the kingdom of Walt Disney's famous screen creations; Snow White, Peter Pan, Alice in Wonderland are all brought to life here and the visit includes a dizzy bobsled ride down the Matterhorn.

Within Hancock Park is sited the George C. Page (La Brea Discoveries) Museum, with its lovely ornamental gardens shown left.

Adjacent to the George C. Page Museum are the La Brea Tarpits *above left where excavations have revealed a wealth of fossilized bones of pre-historic animals which roamed the region some 40,000 years ago. Life-size statues of some of the beasts have been constructed on the site which also contains a typical excavation pit where the bones ha been left intact.*

The city's many outstanding architectural designs include the new Los Angeles County Art Museum *above, which is ringed by magnificent reflecting pools; the* Century Plaza and Schubert Theater *right; the* Post Office *below; the forecourt of the* Bank of America, *with its water fountain and exciting sculpture* center left, *and the* Public Library *below left, flanked by the Union Bank and Bonaventure Hotel.*

By night L.A.'s exciting city skyline above and below left and above right *shimmers against t backdrop of a darkening sky, as myriad lights gleam over the vast metropolis.*

The Harbor Freeway above and right *curves around the city leaving trails of blazing lights, while* top center Crocker Bank towers above t gleaming fountain.

Creating stark silhouettes as the sun sets on the horizon, Watts Towers below *stand as a unique memorial to Simon Rodia, an Italian immigrant whose dream was 'to leave something behind in adopted country'. The towers, erected from an assortment of flotsam and jetsam, scavenged fron the city, took him thirty-three years to build and were finally completed in 1954.*

Universal City Studios featured on these pages and overleaf is the largest motion-picture studio in the world, covering over 420 acres of mountainous plateau and valley.

Founded by Carl Laemmle, in 1912, Universal's early films were presented by Erich von Stroheim, a pioneer in realistic film direction, and some of the greatest names in cinema history, including Deanna Durbin, Doris Day, Rock Hudson and Tony Curtis have been associated with the Studio's successful films.

The sprawling film lot includes a variety of sets, such as those of the wild west, a European Street built at a cost of $2 million, the shark from 'Jaws' and a monster make-up show.

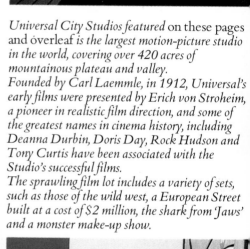

Almost two and a half million visitors are welcomed at Universal each year and the Studio provides a conducted tour of the area, aboard one of the brightly-colored Glamor-Trams, which is usually guided by an aspiring actor or actress.

Lasting about two hours, the tour takes in the entire studio and guests can see at first hand the 'behind the scenes' effects that are realistically presented on celluloid; stunt-men demonstrating their skills, a runaway tram, flash floods and a torpedo attack on one of the man-made lakes.

To end the day in this exciting arena, and perhaps catch a glimpse of one of the movie stars, visitors can head for the Sheraton-Universal deluxe hotel or the Four Stages Restaurant, which is a great place for 'making appearances'.

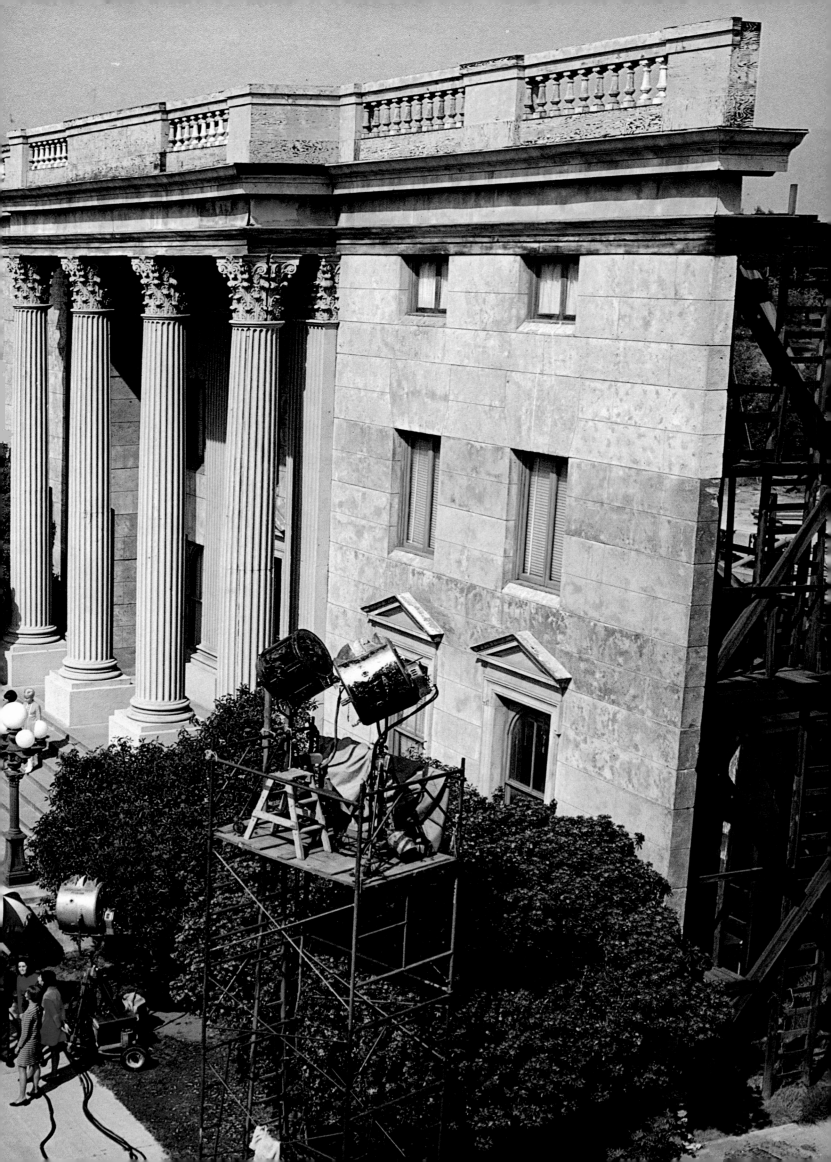

The Freeway Lifestyle

MOST cities of the world have a recognizable center; public transport runs naturally to it, all the big business is there, and it is where most of the excitement happens. Los Angeles is different; its businesses, places of interest and entertainment spots are scattered all over the sprawling metropolis. This makes getting from one place to the other by public transport a tedious and lengthy affair, often requiring several changes of transport. For these reasons, Los Angelenos use their cars more than any other city dwellers in the world, and to accommodate the traffic the Los Angeles authorities have built the most intricate system of city freeways ever seen. These fast six- and eight-lane expressways snake their way about the whole area of metropolitan Los Angeles and out into the state of California.

The whole multi-million-dollar system makes Los Angeles unique among the world's great cities and it also makes the L.A. lifestyle unlike any other. Los Angelenos spend a large part of the day in their cars getting from one place to another within the city and, like the cowboys of the Old West with their horses, they would feel lost without them. Someone once said that Los Angelenos eat, sleep and make love in their cars and one only needs to consider the traffic statistics for the Stack intersection, where four freeways cross at four different levels in northwest L.A., to believe it. More than half a million cars a day pass the Stack, which has become the hub of some 1200 miles of California freeways.

With such vast volumes of traffic, the problems involved in keeping it moving are enormous, and the ever-present hazards of smog or a pile-up can block the freeways for hours. That this does not often happen is a tribute to the design of the freeway system and its clear signposting which keeps the dense, very fast traffic moving smoothly.

There is also a highly sophisticated radio information system controlled by helicopters which keeps drivers constantly informed of conditions ahead.

The evolution of the freeways began in 1940 with the opening of the Pasadena freeway, which runs northwest to the old Spanish town of Pasadena, today a highly desirable residential area. The Pasadena freeway joins three others at the Stack.

Since 1940, the freeways have developed rapidly, many of them following the old railway lines or, when this was not practicable, cutting paths across the city. This was possible only because Los Angeles city grew outwards rather than upwards, so there were no great concentrations of high density building which in other cities would have prevented such drastic treatment.

A major effect of the freeways has been to open up new residential areas and to change the land values of existing estates. Very often the new buildings along freeways are what Los Angelenos call Dingbats: two-story apartment blocks which look thoroughly utilitarian on the freeway side but highly individualistic on their front façades. So today's Los Angelenos betray an attitude to their freeways similar to that of their ancestors toward the railways; while they appreciate them and use them they do not regard them as scenic assets to be viewed from their own homes.

Where there is no housing, the areas round the freeways are landscaped and planted with trees and bushes which absorb noise and traffic fumes. The total effect when seen from the air is of an urban community separated by the wide curving highways which make graceful, green-bordered arabesques through the grid of the city streets. Each enclave enclosed by the freeways becomes separated from other enclaves, though as it generally does not have a central core of its own, or the distinctive neighborhood character found in cities like New York, Paris or London, the Los Angeles 'enclave' is hardly a village or a suburb.

The eclecticism of Los Angeles is a mirror to the world's own, and this makes the freeway city very much a mid-twentieth-century phenomenon. It is not, as some people perhaps would expect, the city of the future – indeed, its Civic Center looks back rather than forward – but it does reflect the absence of one acceptable style and the exploration of all possible styles, that is a feature of much modern design. Los Angeles, like the world today, is an area of experiment where the individual is free to follow his own bent in his way of life or in the buildings in which he works, eats and sleeps.

Locked in the coils of its freeway system, which both liberates and controls his existence, the Los Angeleno can say with that typical air of independence and indifference to others' opinions: 'I did it my way'.

The heavily ornamented globe left is suspended from the second-floor ceiling, with its sun-burst dial, in the Los Angeles Public Library which is considered to be one of the finest and most comprehensively stocked libraries in the world.

Los Angeles' famous racing parks are among the most beautiful in the world, many containing tropical gardens, elaborate picnic areas, decorative wildlife and elegant restaurants.

The Santa Anita Park, for example, is set against a dramatic backdrop of rugged mountains and offers both American and European styles of racing, and visitors can also tour the stables in addition to watching the race-meetings and morning workouts. For thoroughbred racing, however, the Hollywood Park Racetrack is superb, with 350 acres spread across landscaped grounds. The summer season at the 'track of the lakes and flowers' is followed by trotting, shown above and below left and below, in which the competing horses are harnessed to lightweight two-wheeled vehicles called sulkies, in which the driver rides.

Griffith Park, the largest city park in the U.S.A., covers over 4,000 largely mountainous acres, which borders on the foothills of the Santa Monica mountain chain. The park contains the Zoo, Planetarium, the Greek Theater and the popular children's attraction, Travel Town, shown above and above, below and center right. Travel Town contains a collection of old retired rail cars, including an old Los Angeles tram and the Stockton Terminal and Eastern Railroad Engine No. 1, which saw more than 85 years of active duty.

Farmers Market above and below *was started in 1934 by a group of independent farmers specializing in high quality produce. Today this lively market has a collection of individual shops and stalls which sell clothing, gifts and curios as well as the colorfully displayed fruit shown above right.*

L.A. *constantly zings with life – by day or night, from basketball in* Lafayette Park *left to a stroll along exciting* Hollywood Boulevard, *the main artery of the movie capital, shown* right and far right.

Knott's Berry Farm and Ghost Town in Buena Park these pages, has over fifty attractions assembled from old mining towns, which bring to life the days of the old wild west.

This fun-packed entertainment park provides a variety of exciting activities, including action features such as mock gun fights, gold panning, spine-tingling rides down Timber Mountain and trips aboard the old Butterfield Stagecoach, as well as rides on a gold train through the tunnels of a man-made mountain.

In Fiesta Village, with its vibrant Mexican atmosphere, visitors can ride on the thrilling Mexican Whip, the Fiesta Wheel and the Happy Sombrero Ride.

The beautiful campus of the University of California at Los Angeles is shown above left at Dixon Plaza and below left as students relax in the sun-dappled lawned grounds. Sited at Westwood, the University is renowned for its research medical center and the famous Bruin athletic teams.

Linking Hollywood with Beverly Hills is Sunset Boulevard featured on this page which is the site of splendid homes, nightclubs, restaurants and the offices of numerous theatrical agents. The two-mile unincorporated section of the boulevard known as the 'Strip' is famous throughout the world for its lavish nightclub atmosphere and has featured prominently in movies and T.V. films.

Los Angelenos

WHETHER the angels of Our Lady, after whom the city of Los Angeles was named, would feel at home in its present life may be debatable but less angelic mortals evidently do, for the population of the city has risen by several hundred percent over the past two decades alone. The magnet that attracts them has two arms: work and climate.

In the beginning of this century, the attractions were the same but the work was in the fruitful fields and valleys of San Fernando, San Gabriel and Orange County and was on farms where wheat and fruit flourished in the warm Californian sun. Today, it is in factories and industrial works.

At first, many came only as visitors in response to the advertising campaigns designed to attract more people to the West. Among them were Iowans whose annual 'picnics' attended by tens of thousands, became an institution for decades. Persuaded by the idyllic natural conditions, many of them stayed and became the farming population that still forms the nucleus of most communities outside the urban area.

After World War I, Los Angeles County began to change as industrial development gathered speed, oil exploration expanded and land was taken over for real estate to house the increasing population. Many farm workers left the land and sought work in the city. In some cases other factors also helped to redistribute the work force; the Japanese, for example, who had always formed the core of the fruit farmers, were sent to detention camps during World War II and when they were released in 1945 did not return to their former occupation.

Long before this, of course, the film industry had been a big factor in the growth of Los Angeles' population. This vast and all-embracing business provided work not only for those actively engaged in making films but for people in almost every other of the city's trades. Builders, caterers, transport companies, and even farmers played their part in the world's most famous industry.

World War II brought another great influx of people into Los Angeles, as aircraft production soared ahead and the port of Los Angeles became the major West Coast departure point for the Pacific theater of war. Troops from all over the United States and from abroad passed through Los Angeles and many of them returned to settle there when the conflict was over.

Today, Los Angeles has a population of over seven million made up of people originating from four main racial groups: the European whites, principally from England, Germany and Italy; the blacks who moved over from other southern states; the Mexicans, who were the original settlers and who have continued to cross the border in search of work; and the Asiatics, the major part of whom are Japanese.

Although some integration has taken place, the cores of the racial groups remain, maintaining their own customs and attitudes to life and identifying themselves with their own communities rather than with the city as a whole.

The separation between the groups is greatest in the case of blacks and whites and extends to the areas in which they live, the schools they attend and the job opportunities open to them. The disadvantageous situation in which the blacks have found themselves led to severe riots in 1965 in the Watts quarter, to the south of the city, where most of the blacks live. During the riots more than thirty people were killed and more than a thousand injured, while property damage was estimated at some forty million dollars.

Los Angelenos of Mexican origin feel similarly handicapped. Most of them live in East Los Angeles in old, run-down houses and suffer the same limited educational and job opportunities as the blacks; nor, unlike blacks, do they have any representation on the city council. This, too, produces a violent kickback which is one of the city's modern problems.

The Japanese-American Los Angelenos of the post-war generation have dealt with their integration problems in another manner. Many of them have found equality with white Los Angelenos by training to enter the professions and have thus achieved positions of eminence and power which has benefited the community as a whole. Moreover, the powerful trading position of their ancestral country in the modern world has helped to create business opportunities for the young Japanese businessmen in Los Angeles. Their success is confirmed by the fine buildings of the quarter known as Little Tokyo which lies between First and Second Streets. This is the business and commercial center of the Japanese-American community and in its shops are the products of Japanese factories, while its restaurants cater to all who enjoy the delicate flavors of Japanese food.

Chinese, Greeks, Irish, French, Chileans, Hawaiians and the peoples of many other nations are represented in the great polyglot community of Los Angeles. Most of them are newcomers to the rapidly expanding city and in a sense are still finding their places in the new community.

The government of the city, under a Mayor and councilmen who are elected for four-year terms, has the task of finding a *modus vivendi* for the varied communities within the city. From the stresses and strains of diverse demands they must find a balance of power and forces which will satisfy the sense of justice of all the Los Angelenos.

The future of the world's fastest growing new metropolis, which is expected to grow to ten million inhabitants by the end of the decade, will hang on the solution of the 'people' problem as much as on the planned development of industrial growth and the protection of the ecological environment.

The simplistic altar table within St Paul's Episcopal Church on Figueroa Street is shown right.

ople flock to the Santa Anita Park Racetrack
Arcadia these pages and overleaf, *not only to*
atch some of the world's top horseraces, but also
the hope of seeing some of the celebrities who
atronize this outstanding race course.
s superb location, at the foot of the San Gabriel
ountains, provides magnificent mountain
enery, while the infield displays a mosaic of
autiful flowers. During the winter racing season
early one million special Santa Anita giant
ansies can ben seen in peak bloom.
f international fame this 'sport of kings' has
sured for the racecourse one of the richest purse
stributions annually in the world.

The Movieland Wax Museum these pages and overleaf is a shrine to some of the greatest stars of the 'Silver Screen'. Realistically carved in life-like wax, the figures are posed in the memorable film sets that are so closely associated with these world famous actors and actresses.

Among those on view are Fred Astaire and Ginger Rogers in the Academy Award winning "Top Hat" above left, Katherine Hepburn and Humphrey Bogart in "African Queen" top center, Rudolph Valentino as "The Sheik" above, Yul Brinner and Deborah Kerr in "The King and I" above right, Julie Andrews in "Mary Poppins" below right, and Paul Newman and Robert Redford in "Butch Cassidy and the Sundance Kid" below.

Adjoining the Museum is the Palace of Living Arts, which features wax displays from such famous paintings as "The Last Supper" shown below left, as well as reproductions of the Venus de Milo and other statues that are on view in the Louvre in Paris.

*urther exhibits include; Clark Gable and Vivien
eigh in "Gone With the Wind" above left, John
Vayne in "Hondo" below left, Mae West in
She Done Him Wrong" top center, Marilyn
Monroe in "Gentlemen Prefer Blondes" above,
lizabeth Taylor as "Cleopatra" top right, Jean.
Iarlow in "Dinner at Eight" center right,
harlie Chaplin in "The Gold Rush" bottom
ght and the French sex-symbol Brigitte Bardot
elow.*

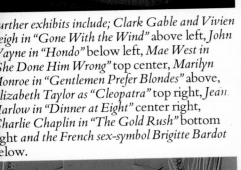

Hollywood

HOLLYWOOD is more than a place on a map. It is a concept which for a while exerted an influence on the world more powerful than that of any king or any philosopher. It also changed the city of Los Angeles from an agricultural center to a world city which attracted the most intelligent, imaginative, and eccentric talent that money could buy and in which power, possessions and money became the name of the game.

In spite of, or perhaps because of, this Hollywood acquired a glamor that has never before in history been so widespread, for none of the great cities of the past were the subject of continual exposure in the mass media.

Today, some of the glamor has become tarnished but the ghosts linger on in the places whose names are as familiar to movie-goers as their own backyard. Grauman's Chinese Theater, now Mann's, may have lost its aura as the temple of the great premieres but it is still the place for first nights. If there are no longer any stars of the stature of Gable and Garbo, the imprints of the hands and feet of the Hollywood greats remain, like the marks on the caves at Altamira and Lascaux, to arouse wonder and awe. By what strange magic, one wonders, did these mortals command such godlike power?

The answer lies in Hollywood itself, a small community established by a God-fearing teetotaller at the turn of the century, whose aim was to provide housing for the farmers and other folk who were arriving in Los Angeles. At about this time, the film industry had begun to take its first faltering steps in New York but restrictions imposed by the patent holders of the new film-making apparatus drove some independent producers West to start work in a studio on Sunset Boulevard.

In California, these men found the kind of weather that made outdoor filming possible – hardly the case today with the Los Angeles smog – and they began to turn out films that spread the name of Hollywood throughout the world.

As the studios developed, the technique of manufacturing box-office hits became highly sophisticated. Actors and actresses were groomed for stardom, the best writers in the land were engaged to write the scripts, often so many of them that the final results were the works of committees rather than individual talents, and every aspect of the job of film-making became a specialized technology. Ruling the film kingdom were the film producers and financiers, men with the tyrannical power of dictators who knew that half the world was listening to them. In the end they were overthrown by the gods and goddesses whom they had created, for the big stars, confident of the appeal of their names, began to form their own film companies, and so the system broke up.

Before this occurred, however, the Hollywood myth had been created by a vast publicity machine which ensured that movie-goers everywhere in the world were constantly reminded of everything that happened in the movie kingdom. The publicity made the stars' lives as

familiar as that of the public's own families, and the places where they foregathered became even more famous than the locations of historical events that have changed the history of the world. The charisma of those shrines, revived by Hollywood's new success as a television film production center, still brings millions of tourists to Hollywood.

They come to walk along Hollywood Boulevard, where bronze medallions commemorate the names of well-known actors of radio and television as well as the films. They sit at the famous intersection at Vine, no longer the meeting place of stars but of the successors to the beatnik cult, and they stop at the famous Brown Derby restaurant which, with its bizarre bowler-hatted shape, still attracts celebrities.

Farther west along the Boulevard is Highland Avenue which leads to the Hollywood Bowl, the great amphitheater in the hills where the Los Angeles Philharmonic holds its summer concerts 'under the stars' and which is crowded every Easter for the impressive Easter Sunrise Service.

Near Highland Avenue is the Wax Museum where one can see the stars, from Shirley Temple to Marilyn Monroe, frozen in some characteristic pose, and examine some of the props used in famous movies. The Museum also shows wax figures of Presidents of the United States, though they attract less interest than the stars.

The Chinese Theater, built by Sid Grauman on the Boulevard, was a follow-up to the Egyptian Theater in the image of a Theban palace, and it is still a piece of architectural showmanship well in keeping with the fantasy world of Hollywood.

Parallel to Hollywood Boulevard runs Sunset Boulevard which cuts through Hollywood to Beverly Hills and the famous Beverly Hills Hotel in its sixteen acres of parkland. A star in its own right, for it has appeared in many films, the Hotel has known innumerable famous guests from the world of international politics as well as of the arts. Sunset Boulevard, forever associated in movie-goers' minds with the film starring Gloria Swanson, is the spine off which spring the roads leading up the canyons in which the more secluded homes of the stars are built. Also on the Boulevard is the famous Strip, the focal point of nightclubs once frequented by the great stars and where their every action was relayed by the movie gossips to the world at large.

The Hollywood touch has literally colored the whole of Angeleno life from the cradle to the grave, for its most spectacular monument is Forest Lawn, the world's most mind-blowing cemetery. Here, in over 200 acres, there are no tombstones but a collection of five hundred statues including copies of the work of Michelangelo and other great sculptors, replicas of famous stained glass windows, copies of famous churches and a theater which gives artistic presentations of paintings of the Crucifixion and Resurrection every half hour. Satirized in Evelyn Waugh's novel 'The Loved One' Forest Lawn nevertheless interprets a concept of death as real in its way as the idealized version of life projected by the movies.

Disneyland's most famous character, Mickey Mouse is shown left.

Disneyland, Walt Disney's famous "Magic Kingdom" built on 150 beautifully landscaped acres, is one of the world's most colorful extravaganzas. For young and old alike there is a wealth of attractions: Dixieland bands *above right*, rides over Fantasyland on Dumbo the Flying Elephant *below right*, turreted Sleeping Beauty Castle *below*, the Mark Twain Riverboat *above* and the exciting Monorail *left which tours the park's perimeter.*

The biggest attraction in California, the charm of Disneyland these pages and overleaf, lies in its make-believe magic – an enchanted park where some of Walt Disney's best-loved characters are brought to life and where it is possible to explore a Peter Pan world that never grows old.

Pirate ships and magic castles, riverboat rides that cruise through swampy jungles and breathtaking adventures that whirl through 'liquid space' on underwater cruises to the North Pole in the Submarine Voyage.

So many exciting things to do and see in the seven themed lands of Main Street, Adventureland, New Orleans Square, Bear Country, Frontierland, Fantasyland and Tomorrowland, with their fun-packed special entertainments, guaranteed to keep the young wide-eyed and adults spell-bound.

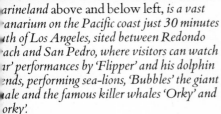

...arineland above and below left, *is a vast
...anarium on the Pacific coast just 30 minutes
...uth of Los Angeles, sited between Redondo
...ach and San Pedro, where visitors can watch
...ar' performances by 'Flipper' and his dolphin
...ends, performing sea-lions, 'Bubbles' the giant
...ale and the famous killer whales 'Orky' and
...orky'.*

*...the giant salt water tank huge turtles, giant
...ss, sharks and many other exotic fish are hand-
...d by a diver – watched by an audience through
...e tank's 170 windows.*

*...is fabulous Oceanarium's attractions also
...clude otters, octopuses, alligators, jewel tanks
...arming with eels, Humboldt penguins and
...lruses captured in the Bering Straits.*

*...e Los Angeles Zoo, in Griffith Park, has an
...rivalled collection of wildlife as well as the
...ore familiar flamingoes, gorillas, elephants and
...lar bears shown on these pages.*

*...imals are exhibited by origin, in natural habitat
...tings, in the five geographical areas of Africa,
...urasia, Australia and North and South
...nerica.*

*...wide variety of birds find nearly natural homes
...one of the world's largest bird farms, while in the
...scinating Children's Zoo there is a sea-lion pool,
...ursery center for newborn animals and their
...others, and a Prairie Dog Village.*

*...e Zoo's efforts in the protection of endangered
...imals has earned it a high reputation for the
...nservation of wildlife.*

On the Town

LOS ANGELES was, and still is, a city full of celebrities, both visiting and resident, and it is also a city of visitors hoping to catch a glimpse of the famous. In the days when Hollywood was young and Los Angeles was small, the celebrity-hunting game would often produce a sighting as a reward for an evening's stalking. Today the size of the city provides welcome anonymity for the famous and frustrates those who seek them.

One solution to the visiting fans' problem which has proved popular has been the development of a series of tours of the city and of the film and television studios. Among them are tours of Universal Studios, the Burbank (Warner Brothers and Columbia) tour, and tours of the CBS and NBC television networks. During any of these the lucky visitor may well come across stars and celebrities on the sets.

Privacy is the keynote of the lives of the famous today and the dedicated fan has to know where to find his stars. The most likely territory for a successful safari is among the hotels and restaurants that provide the right blend of privacy and exposure to ensure that the celebrities are not molested, but at the same time enjoy the feeling that they are not forgotten.

High on the list of such places are the great hotels of Los Angeles where the highest standards of hotel amenities are combined with a splendid array of excellent restaurants where the great names of films, television, and politics can feel suitably pampered.

Almost every celebrity that one can think of in the world of jet-set politicians and entertainers, from the Emperor Hirohito to Frank Sinatra, seems to have stayed either at the Beverly Hills Hotel or The Beverly Wilshire. It is not to be wondered at, as both hotels have all the palatial glamor that is associated with Hollywood. The former is a green and pink mansion set in sixteen acres of parkland and the latter, more in the style of the great European hotels, has many features actually imported from Europe, including chandeliers, mosaics and even gaslights brought from the streets of Scotland's capital, Edinburgh.

These hotels in the traditional style are in stark contrast to more recently built ones, whose design reflects the Space Age. Such a one is the Bonaventure, in downtown Los Angeles. Its huge cylindrical towers stand amid the surrounding buildings like the gantries of a launch site for interstellar journeys and the elevators which crawl up and down the outside of the building look like bubble capsules built to transport passengers to their space vehicle.

The skilfully planned Botanical Gardens overleaf are part of a 207-acre estate created by the pioneer rail tycoon, Henry E. Huntingdon, whose collection of rare books and manuscripts, and priceless works of art are beautifully exhibited in the Library and Art Gallery within the grounds. One of the garden's special features is the Cactus garden left where some 25,000 desert plants are magnificently displayed.

Built by John Portman of San Francisco Hyatt Regency fame, the Bonaventure has five restaurants, including a revolving rooftop 'Top of Five' of high renown. Though a newcomer to the world of great hotels, its unique design and comprehensive services may help to establish it in the top ranks of the hotel world.

Not unexpectedly, the most famous restaurants in Los Angeles are in Hollywood, with the greatest concentration in West Hollywood on Cienaga Avenue, also known as Restaurant Row, and in Beverly Hills. Here French, Italian, English and Scandinavian cuisines and decors share the honors among those restaurants patronized by the top people in politics and the arts.

To most movie fans, no restaurant will be as famous as the Brown Derby and it is still there on Wilshire Boulevard, though now there is another at North Vine Street, with red booths and candlelight, providing intimate meals for people who want to eat incognito. Other restaurants with movie-star associations of the past are Butterfield's, once Errol Flynn's home and now an intriguing natural foods restaurant, and the legendary Schwabs drugstore on Sunset Boulevard, where hopeful actresses arriving in Hollywood hoped to be spotted, like Lana Turner, by some discerning agent, producer, or director. As in so many Hollywood legends, this just does not happen, but the glamor of Schwabs lingers on.

There are over five hundred restaurants in Los Angeles, offering a limitless variety of food ranging through all the European cuisines to the Pacific and Latin American. Any night out in L.A. begins, therefore, with the problem of choosing from a bewildering array of possibilities.

Perhaps fortunately, the problem of what to do after dinner is less acute, for Los Angeles' nightlife is, surprisingly, rather limited considering the size of the metropolis, though the increasing numbers of tourists who come to L.A. from the rest of the United States and overseas has given a spur to some rapid development on the nightclub scene.

Groups, especially jazz and rock and country, provide much of the entertainment and some of the best are to be found along Sunset and Santa Monica Boulevards. In summer, the beach resorts come into their own and big-name bands play along the coast. One of the most long-lived of the seaside jazz places is the Lighthouse at Hermosa Beach, where many of the famous names in jazz have appeared.

On the whole, the Angelenos' own attitude to nightlife is informal and entertainment is sought at clubs, bars with music or at discos. Only on visits to the concert halls and theaters of the Music Center downtown is there more formality and it is here, on special occasions, that some of the diamond-studded sparkle and glamor of Hollywood occasions still remain.

Sited at Long Beach, Mary's Gate Village top left is close to the home of the 'Queen Mary', the famous retired ocean liner, which is now preserved as a museum.

This stately ship features on these pages completed her final voyage on December 9, 1967, after a 14,500 mile journey that took her around South America via Cape Horn, and was purchased by the City of Long Beach at a cost of $3 million.

The liner's attractions include a three-level panorama created across the lower decks which reveals the world's largest marine exhibition, Living Sea exhibits designed by Jacques Cousteau, two malls of shops and three excellent restaurants. Visitors can also tour the section of the liner on the Upper Decks which shows the luxury suites which were in use during her 31 years of Atlantic crossings.

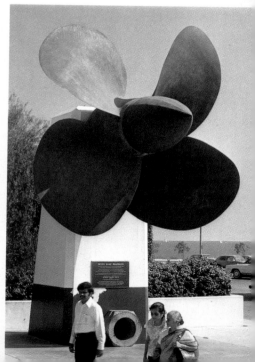

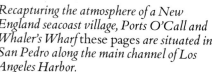

Recapturing the atmosphere of a New England seacoast village, Ports O'Call and Whaler's Wharf these pages are situated in San Pedro along the main channel of Los Angeles Harbor.
Fascinating stores above and center left are filled with attractively displayed merchandise; Colonial style shops and restaurants below left, with their quaint tavern signs and small-paned windows, line cobblestone streets, and in the harbor fishing boats, yachts and tuna clippers pass in and out in a steady stream.

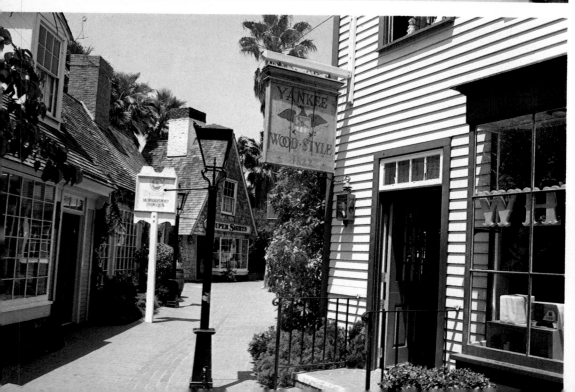

The Beaches of L.A.

HOWEVER smogbound Los Angeles becomes, there is always an escape and Los Angelenos make the best of it. Every day of the year the cars speed along the freeways headed for the coast where the sun shines summer and winter, except for the occasional storm, and where, even in winter, there are wetsuit-clad surfers riding the big Pacific waves and yachts scudding over the sea off-shore with colorful jibs billowing out like flowers.

Due west of Hollywood lie the resorts where the stars have built their seaside homes, creating the Californian version of the Côte d'Azur with smart houses and clubs. Some ingenious developers even tried to recreate the atmosphere of Venice and Naples. Hollywood's Venice near Santa Monica had lagoons, bridges, columned porticoes and even gondolas to provide the right atmosphere, but the dream city was no match for the oil industry whose wells eventually took over the whole unlikely scene. Naples still survives in the south near Long Beach, a quiet little backwater with tall palm trees and bungalows reminiscent of many an Italian town but it, too, has lost some of its original conviction.

Santa Monica is the biggest of the resorts, and is a bustling town with wide boulevards and a palm-lined promenade reminiscent of Mediterranean resorts. It has a large population, many of them commuters to Los Angeles, and was the point at which the city originally began to spread to the sea. In 1870, there was only a handful of houses at the exit of the Santa Monica Canyon and it did not occur to anyone then that the city would have extended its western limits as far as the seashore a hundred years later. The attractions of the coast, coupled with the worldwide fashion for going to the seaside for health and pleasure, awoke turn-of-the-century Los Angelenos to the fact that the long sandy beaches and rocky headlands were ideal places in which to live. Improvements in local transport brought the coast closer and the development of the beachfront gathered speed.

The suburbs, or 'surfurbs' as they have been called, spread southwards past Santa Monica Pier, built in the style of the British piers and still a center of entertainment, to Marina del Rey, a huge artificial harbor providing moorings for thousands of boats. This vast port has shopping centers and restaurants and Undersea Gardens where all sorts of exotic fish can be seen through viewing windows under the water level.

Past the Los Angeles airport at Dockweiler State Beach, the sands continue, separated by a pedestrian and cyclists' promenade from rows of small frame houses which make an individual and picturesque backdrop to the beach.

To the Los Angeleno, the beach spells freedom to be himself, to cultivate idiosyncratic styles of dress and houses if he wants to. Here at the shore, he feels he is a free man and can do as he likes. The great symbol of L.A. man at the beach is the surfboard. Stacked along the promenades, stuck in the sand like neolithic emblems, decorated with tribal markings, surfboards are everywhere, like an invasion armada preparing to set off across the Pacific.

Around the Palos Verdes Peninsula, a rocky headland with a fine fifteen-mile scenic drive, the surfboards vanish. Two old lighthouses attest to its danger for ships in the days of sail, and a Marineland Oceanarium has a fine collection of sea creatures which are literally put through the hoop to entertain the customers.

Round the peninsula, on a south-facing shore, are the Port of Los Angeles and Long Beach which together make up the world's largest man-made harbor, and one of the world's busiest ports. There are over fifty miles of quays, docks and waterfront protected by a breakwater. The ships that call here bring or take away cargoes from all over the world.

Long Beach is a naval base as well as an industrial city and pleasure resort, and numbers among its attractions one of the world's most famous ships, the *Queen Mary*. When this splended Transatlantic Cunarder came to the end of her useful life she was saved from the scrapheap by the City of Long Beach and is moored in the port today, where she serves as a hotel, restaurant and museum organized by the famous Jacques Cousteau. To keep her company, the *Queen Mary* has two Canadian ships, the *Princess Louise* and her sister ship which bears the same name nearby.

This rocky, indented island of Catalina is almost custom-made as a place to let one's romantic feelings about the sea run free. It was once a hideout for smugglers and pirates, it is wild and thinly inhabited, and its main port, Avalon, retains the end-of-century charm it had when it was built in 1887 to provide hospitality for passengers on the first steamer services.

Apart from its beauty, Catalina's claim to fame is that it was the home of Zane Grey, whose house is now a hotel. The writer's stories of big game fishing and the early days of the West embody in their romantic attitude something of the spirit not only of Catalina Island but of the whole American West in which Los Angeles and its coast have played a continuing and evolving role.

The star-spangled banner and flag of California flutter outside the dome of the Beverly Hills Hall left.

Hollywood Bowl left, is the world's most beaut
natural amphitheater, located in Cahuenga Pa
above Hollywood. Created in the early 1920's,
stage and shell look out over tier upon tier of sea
fashioned Greek style.

The Bowl, with its perfect, natural acoustics,
draws thousands of music devotees in the summ
who can enjoy a wealth of musical programs fro
symphonies to pop music.

Home of the Los Angeles Philharmonic Orches
performances at the theater include the famous
'Symphonies Under the Stars', and internationa
known conductors and soloists can be seen in the
classical programs which take place on Tuesday,
Thursday and Saturday nights.

As well as the enjoyment of the music visitors to
this superb theater can also relish the dazzling
vista of the Hollywood hills which spread like a
vast panorama when viewed from the seats high
on the hill.

The magnificent aerial view above shows the
sprawling metropolis of Los Angeles fanning out
from a misty blue horizon.

bulous Beverly Hills, with its magnificent
aza overleaf, boasts its own City Hall which
een above amid lovely terraced gardens filled
th a profusion of colorful blooms.

e palm-lined Danon Drive shown right at
sk is just one of the splendid thoroughfares in
s 'home of the stars' which contains some of the
st picturesque glens, canyons and hillsides,
th a wealth of beautiful homes.

sadena, sited at the foothills of the Sierra
adre mountain range in the San Gabriel
lley, lies eleven miles northwest of the
wntown district of Los Angeles. Its charming
ity Hall is pictured below.

Although the majority of the wax figures on display at the Hollywood Wax Museum, on Hollywood Boulevard these pages, feature celebrities and movie stars from the entertainment world, non-entertainment personalities are also included in the 200 mannequins which show former U.S. Presidents amid religious figures.

International stars include right Farrah Fawcett Majors, from the highly successful television series 'Charlie's Angels', Sammy Davis Jnr, and Elvis Presley.

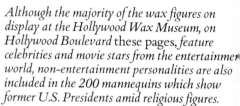

Marilyn Monroe, seen below in her famous dress-blowing scene from 'The Seven-Year Itch', is one of the Museum's most publicized figures, and other famous personalities include Henry Winkler as 'The Fonz' with O.J. Simpson below left, Mae West left, Bob Hope and Bing Crosby above left and Mohammed Ali above.

The Museum also contains a Chamber of Horrors similar to Madame Tussaud's in London, which includes some of the macabre scenes from horror-movies, and an added attraction is the Oscar Movie Theater which presents a film spanning more than four decades of Academy Award Winners and presentations.

Sunny, pleasure-filled Los Angeles has long draw
visitors to this dynamic metropolis where the
excitement of the city is ever evident and the fun
'The Big Orange' is always ready to be tasted.

For visitors to Los Angeles there is always a mult
of ways to fill the long, warm days as these pages
show – roller skating, cycling, fishing and chess –
well as the fabulous sights in and around this vita
or perhaps a glimpse of fortunes to come will be
revealed by an expert in astrology and palmistry!

SEE YOUR
PHOTO. MADE
IN ONE MINUTE!
WITH FOOTPRINTS OF FAMOUS STARS ★

SANDRA
ASTROLOGY
CARDS
CRYSTAL
HAND WRITING
READINGS

To the west of Los Angeles lies the Pacific Ocean with its beautiful resort communities bordered by miles of sandy beaches which are washed by the Ocean's rolling waves.

Santa Monica, seen above right as dusk silhouettes the lonely palms, is considered to have one of the finest beach areas in Southern California, and its Pier below right draws fun-seekers who can enjoy the excellent fishing, boating and swimming facilities.

Fabulous Malibu overleaf, noted for its famous movie colony, stretches along the West Pacific Coast Highway, from the Los Angeles city line to the extreme frontier of Ventura County. Its wide, smooth beaches delight thousands of visitors who flock yearly to idly bathe in the sun, go boating or swim in this sunshine paradise.

Venice below left, an oceanside community south of Santa Monica, was founded with the intention of resembling its namesake in Italy. One of its picturesque canals is shown below, while the mural above attracts comment on its unusual desert scene.

Newport Beach and Balboa these pages, sited so
35 miles south of Los Angeles, nests on a sandy bea
strip opening onto the Pacific. This fashionable aq
city attracts not only the wealthy and famous who
moor their boats in the resort's ports, but also sights
and enthusiastic fishermen.

The beautifully tempting beach of Malibu is seen
again overleaf gently lapped by azure waters.

First published in Great Britain 1979 by Colour Library International Ltd.
© Illustrations: Colour Library International Ltd., 163 East 64th St., New York, N.Y. 10021.
Colour separations by La Cromolito, Milan, Italy.
Display and text filmsetting by Focus Photoset, London, England.
Printed and bound by SAGDOS - Brugherio (MI), Italy.
ISBN 0-8317-5639-X Library of Congress Catalogue Card No. 79-2123
Published in the United States of America by Mayflower Books, Inc., New York City
Published in Canada by Wm. Collins and Sons, Toronto